"Thank God the East Surreys are there"

The East Surrey Regiment in World War I

© *National Football Museum*

by

John Dewhurst

Foreword by Colonel (Rtd) Patrick Crowley, DL

Second Edition published in Great Britain 2025

Amazon Kindle Publishing

The right of John Dewhurst to be identified as the author of this book has been asserted by him in accordance with the Copyright, Designs and Patents Act 1988.

Copyright © John Dewhurst 2021 & 2025

British Library Cataloguing in Publication Data

A catalogue record for this book is available from the British Library.

ISBN: 9798310768383

All rights reserved. No part of this publication may be reproduced, stored in a retrieval system or transmitted, in any form, or by any means, electronic, mechanical, photocopying, recording or otherwise, without prior permission

Contents

Preface

Dedication

Acknowledgements and thanks

Foreword

Introduction

Chapter 1: August 1914: The Regiment goes to War

Chapter 2: August 1914: The East Surreys at the battle of Mons

Chapter 4: The 2nd Battalion: India to Salonika via the Western Front

Chapter 5: 1915: The Defence of Hill 60

Chapter 6: 1916: Into battle with footballs!

Chapter 7: Armistice: The East Surrey Regiment on 11th November 1918

Chapter 8: 1919: The East Surreys in Russia

Conclusion

Preface

This book originated in a series of articles written between 2014 and 2019 for *'Saints Alive'*, the parish magazine of All Saints Church in Kingston-upon-Thames. The church, which has stood for centuries in the centre of this ancient town, has a long association with the East Surrey Regiment and houses its Regimental Memorial Chapel, along with many individual commemorations of members of the Regiment. The various chapters of the book are, with the exception of the final chapter, re-worked versions of the *'Saints Alive'* articles, together with some additional material. The first article was written to commemorate the centenary of the 1st Battalion's involvement in the first action of the War at the battle of Mons, which was also marked by a special service at All Saints at 12.00 noon on 23rd August 2014, the exact centenary of the first engagement. The Order of Service is included in this booklet as an Appendix.

Following the article's favourable reception amongst the extensive *'Saints Alive'* readership it was decided, in consultation with the Vicar and the Editor, to follow it up with an occasional series that would follow the Regiment through the four years of the conflict, culminating in a final article explaining where each Battalion was at the moment of the Armistice at 11.00am on 11th November 1918 and how the news of the end of hostilities was received by the troops.

The various articles drew heavily on the East Surrey Regiment's Battalion War Diaries, which are available online thanks to the painstaking efforts of the members of the Queens Royal Surrey Regimental Association who laboriously transcribed the typewritten originals in order to make the diaries widely available to military historians and general readers alike. In the interests of authenticity, any errors in spelling, grammar and punctuation which were transcribed from the original diaries have been retained.

The Holy Trinity Chapel, All Saints Church, Kingston upon Thames

The Memorial Chapel of the East Surrey Regiment

Acknowledgements and thanks

Many individuals and organisations have contributed in some way to this booklet, and I am hugely grateful and deeply indebted to all of them. They include:

The Vicar and Churchwardens of All Saints Church, Kingston-upon-Thames; Isabel Isaacson, Editor, *'Saints Alive'*, All Saints Church (who also proof-read the final draft of the text); Colonel (Retired) Patrick Crowley DL, Deputy Colonel (Heritage), The Princess of Wales Royal Regiment; Colonel (Retired) Tony Ward DL and the Friends of the Surrey Infantry Museum; Steve Johnson, former Manager of The Surrey Infantry Museum, Woking, especially for drawing my attention to Captain Adams's personal diary of the 1919 North Russia campaign (see Chapter 8); The Surrey History Museum, Woking; The Princess of Wales's Royal Regiment and the Queen's Regiment Museum, Dover Castle; The National Football Museum, for permission to use the illustration of the 8th Battalion's 'Football Charge'; The Imperial War Museum, for permission to use an extract from the *'Voices of the First World War'* website; Alastair Deller, for permission to reproduce the photograph that appears at the end of the Conclusion; and The Queen's Royal Surrey Regimental Association, for permission to make use of extensive extracts from the on-line Battalion War Diaries, together with other material from the website.

Finally, but by no means least, to my wife Julia, who has tolerated the virtual billeting of the East Surrey Regiment in our home for upwards of six years with her customary grace and gentle good humour, and who has read and commented on the text of the booklet at the various stages of its development with enormous insight and perceptiveness.

This book is dedicated to the 6,684 men of the East Surrey Regiment who did not come home.

"Thank God the East Surreys are there."

General Sir John French, April 1915

Foreword

It is a huge honour to write the Foreword for this book, both as a Deputy Lieutenant for the County of Surrey and as a Deputy Colonel of The East Surrey Regiment's successor, The Princess of Wales's Royal Regiment (PWRR). Infantry regiments have changed shape over the centuries, from being called after their commander or colonel, as the East Surreys were, raised as 'Villiers' Marines' in 1702, to be numbered as a Regiment of the Line and then, eventually, associated with a county. The East Surrey Regiment inherited the heritage of both the 31st Regiment of Foot and the 70th Regiment of Foot in 1881, and had very strong connections with both the barracks and All Saints Church in Kingston upon Thames.

The 'other' Surrey regiment was The Queen's Royal West Surrey Regiment. Both regiments were amalgamated in 1959 to become The Queen's Royal Surrey Regiment, then in 1966 formed The Queen's Regiment from the infantry regiments of Surrey, Sussex, Kent and Middlesex, before the most recent amalgamation in 1992 with The Royal Hampshire Regiment, forming the PWRR. The new regiment has inherited the traditions of all its forebears, including The East Surrey Regiment, and still recruits many of its soldiers from East Surrey.

The East Surrey Regiment had seventy-eight years of very distinguished service, dominated, of course, by the First and Second World Wars. The First World War is focused on in this important booklet, expertly pulled together by John Dewhurst. East Surrey soldiers served in most of the conflict areas, as regulars, reservists, Kitchener volunteers and conscripts. The East Surreys raised nineteen battalions, of which most saw active service and fought courageously; however, the Regiment lost 6,684 officers and other ranks killed. As the centenary of the Great War has come to an end, John has done a great service to those brave East Surrey soldiers, bringing their memory alive and remembering their achievements. Their names are remembered in the two Books of Remembrance, which are kept safely in glass cases in the Regimental Chapel of All Saints Church.

Colonel (Retd) Patrick Crowley DL

Introduction

The East Surrey Regiment was formed in 1881 by the amalgamation of the 31st (Huntingdonshire) and 70th (Surrey) Regiments of Foot, together with the 1st and 3rd Regiments of the Royal Surrey Militia. The Regimental Depot was at Kingston Barracks. Following a series of reorganisations of the British Army that began in 1959, the Regiment is now part of the Princess of Wales's Royal Regiment.

The East Surrey Regiment was heavily involved in the many battles of the First World War, from the first action of the British Expeditionary Force at Mons in August 1914, until the Armistice on 11th November 1918. The Regiment expanded enormously during the war years, from its initial complement of two regular battalions and a third home-based training battalion to nineteen battalions, comprising along with the Regular battalions and two Special Reserve battalions, four Territorial Army and twelve 'New Army' (or 'Special Service') units, including four London Regiment battalions that were 'cap badged' to the East Surrey Regiment for the duration of the war.

After four long years of bitter fighting, the Allied forces emerged victorious, but at a terrible cost. The enormously high price of victory was massively felt by the Regiment. Almost seven-thousand of the men who served with the East Surreys did not come home following the cessation of hostilities. It is an utterly mind-numbing statistic.

This book does not set out to provide a comprehensive historical account of the Regiment's involvement in the war. Instead, it highlights a number of key episodes: the deployment of the 1st Battalion as part of the British Expeditionary Force in August 1914; the battle of Mons; the first Christmas in the trenches; the recall of the 2nd Battalion from its peacetime station in India for service in the bloodbath of the battle of Ypres; the action at the Hohenzollern Redoubt; the defence of Hill 60, where the 1st Battalion won three VCs in a single day, along with several other decorations for gallantry; and the famous episode during the first day of the battle of the Somme, when men of the 8th (Service) Battalion advanced into no-man's land between the trenches kicking footballs in front of them. A final chapter, which has not appeared in *'Saints Alive',* recounts the involvement of the 1st Battalion in the ill-fated and almost entirely forgotten Allied military intervention in the Russian Civil War in 1919.

Chapter 1

August 1914 - The Regiment goes to War

A large processional banner made from golden silk hangs in the Holy Trinity Chapel of All Saints Church, the Memorial Chapel of the East Surrey Regiment. A small wooden plaque on the banner's staff is inscribed:

> To the Glory of God and in memory
>
> Of the heroic deeds of the 1st East
>
> Surrey Regiment with the first seven
>
> Divisions in 1914 this banner was originally
>
> worked and given for the commemoration
>
> festival at the Albert Hall 14th December 1916
>
> (by those who hold their bravery dear)

The banner is embroidered with the East Surrey Regimental crest and an inscription which includes reference to the former 31st Regiment of Foot from which the 1st Battalion of the East Surreys was formed in 1881. The inscription on the banner reads:

East Surrey

XXXI

August – Nov 1914

The 1st Battalion of the East Surreys was engaged in the Great War from the very outset, as part of the 14th Infantry Brigade of the 5th Division of the British Expeditionary Force. The Regiment's 2nd Battalion was stationed in India at the outbreak of war and did not return to England until December 1914, from where it was posted to Salonika, via Egypt, in October 1915. The 3rd and 4th (Reserve) Battalions were training units based at the regiment's Kingston depot.

The comparatively small British Expeditionary Force (BEF) consisted initially of just four divisions, compared with French and German field armies that were almost twenty times larger. Commanded by Sir John French, the BEF was composed entirely of professional long-service regular soldiers and well-trained reservists. The Fifth Division was one of two that made up the Second Army Corps under the command of General Sir Horace Smith-Dorrien. The First Army Corps was commanded by General Sir Douglas Haig. The BEF became known to posterity as 'The Old Contemptibles' after the German Kaiser had allegedly referred to it as 'a contemptible little army'.

When the general mobilization of the Army was ordered late on 4th August 1914 following the declaration of war on Germany, the 1st Battalion was stationed at the Curragh Camp, near Dublin, where the 14th Brigade (consisting, along with the East Surreys, of the 1st Battalion of the Duke of Cornwall's Light Infantry and the 2nd Battalions of the Suffolk Regiment and the Manchester Regiment) had been posted for some time. The imminent threat of armed insurrection in Ireland was by far the overriding British political and military preoccupation during the first part of 1914, regardless of simmering tensions on the continent.

The Battalion War Diary records that on 6th August the Battalion's relatively modest peacetime establishment was supplemented by the arrival of 402 reservists from the Kingston depot at 4.00pm in the afternoon, with a further 242 arriving at 6.00am the next morning. A final batch of thirty reservists arriving early on 8th August brought the Battalion up to its full wartime establishment of 30 officers and 992 other ranks. The logistical complexities of this operation in an era of relatively primitive communications, and only one of the many which were taking place simultaneously throughout the country, can only be wondered at.

The few days before the scheduled embarkation for France were spent in fitting-out, shooting practice in the rifle butts and route-marching to get the men, and especially the inevitably unfit reservists, conditioned for the days of hard foot-slogging that lay ahead. The War Diary for 11th August records:

> *'Battn. Marched by train loads about 10 miles. Many Reservists found to have badly fitting boots probably due to submission of incorrect returns to OC records on transfer to Army Reserve. As far as possible these boots were changed'.*

The Battalion set sail from Dublin's Alexander Basin on the evening of Saturday 13th August after several delays, *'destination unknown'* as the War Diary records, but actually for Le Havre. The Diary continues*:*

> *'Many Dublin friends turned out both in streets and at the Dock to give the Battalion a send-off and placed on board a packet of fruit, cake and cigarettes for each man'.*

After spending an uncomfortable Sunday 14th August at sea (the War Diary records that cooking arrangements aboard ship were 'inadequate', with no facilities even for boiling water), disembarkation arrangements the following day at Le Havre were reported to have worked well. Following a rest break at the dockside, the Battalion marched off to its allocated camp for the night. It began to rain heavily, reducing the camp and the surrounding roads to a quagmire, and the next day, Tuesday 16th August, had to be spent in 'drying out'. The Battalion then entrained with the battalions of the other three regiments that made up the 14th Brigade very early the next morning, leaving Le Havre railway station at 3.00am and trundling north at a painfully slow 20 mph via Amiens to Le Cateau, which was reached early in the evening of Thursday 18th August. From there (they would be back, although, as Chapter 2 explains, in very different circumstances) the men marched to Landrecies, close to the Belgian border. A junior officer of the 14th Brigade wrote of this first march:

> 'It turned out to be a good ten miles, and our weary reservists found it hard to keep up. Many fell out, and we were beat by the time we got to our billets at 1.00am'.

The Brigade crossed the frontier at 9.00am on Monday 22nd August, having set off from its billets at 5.00am, and its assigned position near the village of Les Herbieres was reached at 3.00pm that afternoon.

The Brigade was responsible for a strategically important section of the Mons-Conde Canal that was crossed by a road bridge and a railway bridge, both of which would be vital objectives for the German advance. The hot eighteen-mile march had been *'... made more trying'*, as the War Diary comments ... *'by the cobbled roads of Belgium'*.

And it was only the beginning.

--ooOoo--

Chapter 2

August 1914 - The East Surreys at the Battle of Mons

The British Expeditionary Force's halt at the Mons Canal was intended to be only a stage in a continuing advance into Belgium. But what the British command was completely unaware of was that the whole German First Army under General von Kluck was very close at hand, wheeling anti-clockwise through Belgium towards the British positions. German military strategy was rooted in the Schlieffen Plan, originally devised by the High Command in 1905. The plan envisaged a rapid advance through Belgium that was designed to encircle Paris from the south. The German commanders were equally unaware of the presence of the BEF, with the morning mists grounding their spotter aircraft and their scouting cavalry somehow failing to observe the British deployments. By the time the East Surreys came into the line, units of the BEF further east towards Mons were already in action, the first shots having been fired at dawn on Saturday 22nd August. The War Diary records that the East Surreys had their first encounter with German forces at 1.00pm on the afternoon of

Sunday 23rd August, when the arrival of German infantry forced them to break off from clearing the ground and digging firing positions to improvise what in military terms is called a 'hasty defence' against the increasingly ferocious massed German assaults.

The coolly understated language of the Battalion War Diary conceals much of what was clearly a desperate fight against enormous odds. The rapid rifle fire of the British infantry was so intense (in what was known as a 'mad minute' a well-trained rifleman could fire off fifteen extremely accurate rounds) that the German troops were convinced that they were facing batteries of machine guns, whereas in fact, each infantry battalion was equipped with only two. The War Diary commended the *'excellent work'* of the Battalion's Machine Gun section from its position on the railway bridge over the canal,

> *'... coupled with the steady firing of the men in the trenches (which) helped much to delay the enemies advance'.*

In fact, not a single German soldier crossed the canal that afternoon, and the advancing forces suffered severe casualties. But at 11.00pm that night the Battalion received the order to pull back because of increasing threats to both its flanks. The retirement, always a potentially difficult battlefield manoeuvre, was evidently disciplined and well-conducted in spite of it being a night-time operation. The bridges in the Battalion's section were systematically blown up by the Brigade's sappers, a laborious and hazardous business in the days before the development of plastic explosives and, as the War Diary records:

> '... the withdrawal to the south of the River Haime was then in accordance with previous instructions received carried out in good order by alternate positions of the line and covered finally by the remainder of the Suffolk Regiment'.

After reporting to Brigade Headquarters at Thulin, the depleted Battalion marched on to Bois de Boussu where it eventually bivouacked in a factory yard at about 2.00am on the morning of 24th August. The men, who must have been completely exhausted, had not eaten a hot meal since very early on the morning of Saturday 22nd August.

The War Diary records two East Surreys as having been killed on this first day of action, with six men wounded and a further 133 missing, many of whom were almost certain to have been fatalities unavoidably left behind in the retreat. By the end of the month, following the epic fighting retreat from Mons in which the East Surreys were assigned the hazardous task of forming a rearguard to protect the Division's continuing retirement, and after a fierce holding action at Le Cateau on 26th August (which was actually a major battle that has been described by the military historian Allan Mallinson as the British Army's most major engagement since Waterloo in 1815[1]) a further three men had been reported killed, with 44 wounded and 182 'missing'

And yet the East Surrey's first fatality of the war had not been the result of enemy action. A poignantly laconic entry in the War Diary for Thursday 18th August records:

> *'Whilst bathing in the canal (at Landrecies) Pte. Walters, C Coy, was drowned'.*

No battle that ends with a strategic withdrawal followed by a 200-mile retreat can reasonably be regarded as a victory. But nor was it a defeat. The BEF withdrew from Mons depleted but in generally good order, having inflicted very heavy casualties on the German army. In spite of its own considerable

---

[1] Mallinson, 2014 p. 415

losses, the BEF lived to fight another day. Together with the holding action at Le Cateau, the battle of Mons succeeded in slowing the momentum of the German advance, adding to the unanticipated delays the Germans already encountered in taking Liege and the other Belgian frontier forts during the first days of their advance.

This loss of momentum contributed very significantly to General von Kluck's fateful decision on 30th August to turn his line of march to the east, across the north of Paris, rather than driving on to encircle the city from the south as the Schlieffen plan had envisaged. Von Kluck's surprising, and since much-debated, manoeuvre provided the regrouped and reinforced Allied forces with the priceless opportunity of striking at the exposed right flank of the German army, which it duly did at the battle of the Marne, fought between 5th and 12th October 1914. The subsequent German retreat to the river Aisne marked the end of the High Command's bid for a decisive victory and thus the failure of the Schlieffen Plan. The subsequent 'race to the sea' and the first battle of Ypres (15th October to 30th November 1914) saw the transformation of the initial 'war of movement' into the deadly and prolonged stagnation of trench warfare. But by end of the first battle of Ypres, over four-fifths of the original BEF had been listed as either killed, wounded or missing.

No-one, it was now clear, was going to be home by Christmas.

--ooOoo--

Chapter 3

December 1914 - Christmas in the Trenches

December 1914 saw the East Surreys deployed in a section of the now more-or-less static Western Front, some 17 miles to the south of the ancient Belgian cloth-manufacturing town of Ypres.

On December 2nd, the Battalion had paraded for inspection by General Sir John French, Commander in Chief of the British Expeditionary Force. The War Diary records the Battalion's strength as 14 officers and 633 other ranks. The Diary contains a verbatim record of the speech General French made to the assembled ranks. He praised the men for the prominent part they had played in the battles which had followed the epic retreat from Mons in late August. Early in September, along with the rest of the 5th Infantry Division, the Battalion had been heavily engaged in the battle of the Marne which succeeded in pushing the German forces away from Paris. Just a week later came the battle of the Aisne, where the BEF took part in the Allied attempts to dislodge the German forces from a strong position on a chalk ridge rising 500 feet above the river. The first battle of Ypres had followed soon after. In short, General French told the men that they had:

> *... crowded into the four months of this campaign enough fighting to fill the Battle Honours of any corps (and greatly added to the fame of a grand old Regiment)'.*

Having spent the early part of December in billets at Neuve Eglise, the Battalion returned to trench duty near Wulverghem on December 10th, relieving the Devon Regiment during the evening in *'very dark and wet weather'*. The Diary records a steady accumulation of casualties from artillery shelling and sniper fire during this period in the front line: two men wounded on the 12th, one killed and three wounded on the 13th (following the arrival of reinforcements consisting of one officer and 160 other ranks), three men killed on the 14th, with a further six wounded, four killed on the 15th and four other ranks killed and 21 wounded on the 16th. In addition to the casualties resulting from enemy action, the Diary comments that casualties from sickness had increased significantly because of the cold and wet conditions. It notes that the trenches had become so waterlogged by continual rain that a pump had to be used in an attempt, only partially successful, to dry them out. And ominously, 'enteric fever' (otherwise known as typhoid) was also making its first appearance amongst the ranks.

At 9.00pm in the evening of 17th December, in very cold and frosty conditions, the Battalion was relieved by the Dorset Regiment and marched back to its billets at St Jans Capel, arriving at 2.30am. It was, the Diary comments, *'rather cold ... very wet and unpleasant',* but in spite of this the Battalion was warned to be on standby *'... to turn out at shortest notice'*. The war was still very close at hand. And on December 19th, a round of inoculations against enteric fever began.

The poor weather did not relent as Christmas approached. Most days seem to have been characterised by rain, fog, hard overnight frost and freezing conditions during daylight hours. On 23rd December the Battalion relocated to Dranoutre in showers of freezing sleet to share billets with the Duke of Cornwall's Light Infantry. The Battalion arrived to find the village and its surrounding roads *'a sea of mud',* with the billets themselves *'very limited and extremely dirty'.* Christmas Eve was spent initially in rapid marching and 'doubling', presumably as a means of counteracting the penetrating cold and damp, then in moving the Battalion's transport into a drier field and in cleaning up the billets, some of which had been condemned by the Medical Officer. Later in the day, a further reinforcement of 108 other ranks joined the Battalion.

Christmas Day dawned with hard frost and freezing fog. The Battalion attended *'Open Air Divine Service'*, during which the Brigadier's greeting was read to the men (and, according to the Diary, *'heartily cheered'*) followed by a distribution of cards from King George and Queen Mary together with *'gifts'* from Princess Mary. *'All'*, the Diary observes *'were much gratified in being thus honoured'*. But there was to be little respite from the war. On 29th December, the Battalion returned to the trenches north-east of Wulverghem in a highly efficient manoeuvre that was carried out, according to the Diary, *'expeditiously and without incident'*. They found their new positions to be absolutely saturated, with water and mud *'of varying depths, in places as much as waist deep'*. And then the remorseless attrition from enemy gunfire resumed; on the 30th December, three men were killed and seven wounded.

--ooOoo--

Chapter 4

The 2nd Battalion: India to Salonika via the Western Front

Amongst the many commemorative plaques that line the wood-panelled walls of the East Surrey Regiment's Memorial Chapel in All Saints Church is one to Capt. Fleming-Sandes of the 2nd Battalion, who won the Victoria Cross as a 2nd Lieutenant on 29th September 1915 at the defence of the Hohenzollern Redoubt during the battle of Loos on the Western Front. The Battalion War Diary describes the episode:

> 'On the morning of 29th September, the enemy made a very determined attack on the South of Little Willie [NB This was a strategically important trench] the company commander Capt. Dowler was severely wounded and the men being very much shaken and owing to shortage of bombs began to retire. Lieut. Fleming-Sandes was sent up and held the enemy. Later the regiments to his right gave way and his men were also inclined to do so, so he rallied his men, jumped on the parapet and drove the enemy back and occupied the original position'.

The East Surrey Regiment's 2nd Battalion was stationed in India when war was declared in August 1914. The Battalion was recalled to Europe almost immediately and was assigned to the 85th Infantry Brigade of the 28th Division. After the long voyage home via the Suez Canal, the Battalion docked at Devonport on 23rd December, and travelled on by train to Magdalen Hill Camp near Winchester. Following an intensive period of fitting-out and training, mobilization was completed on 17th January 1915. The next day, the Battalion marched from Winchester to Southampton Docks (a distance of some 20 miles which, according to the Diary, took them all of five hours following a 7.30am start) and embarked for the six-hour crossing to Le Havre, docking on the afternoon of 19th January. After a short rest break, the Battalion travelled on by rail the following morning via Rouen, Abbeville, Boulogne and Calais to the small market town and railway junction of Hazebrouk just a few miles south-west of Ypres, arriving there at 1.00am on 22nd January.

The Battalion was soon in action in the trenches near Ypres, in the notorious sector that became known as the Ypres Salient. The first casualty, a soldier wounded whilst carrying water and rations up to the fire trenches, was sustained on 4th

February. But there were to be many, many more. On 14th February, advancing over what the Diary describes as *'open and very exposed ground'* in an attempt to recapture a trench that had been lost to the enemy, 'A' and 'C' Companies lost almost all their officers and a very large number of other ranks. Just a few days later, 'B' and 'D' Companies sustained a similarly high proportion of casualties. After just five days of action, only 200 of the Battalion's 1,000 officers and men who had left Southampton remained fit for duty, with many having been either killed or mortally wounded. The remnants of the Battalion were withdrawn to billets at Locre on 19th February for much needed rest, reinforcement and refitting.

The Battalion returned to trench duty at Scotch Farm near Lindenhoek on 4th March. And the casualties soon began to mount once again, not least through a 'friendly fire' incident on 12th March in which a trench held by the Battalion was heavily shelled by the British artillery during an attack. The incident left five officers and 27 other ranks dead. Two weeks later, a hand grenade exploded during practice, killing three men and injuring eleven others. April proved to be even worse. On the 22nd, the Diary recorded a disturbing new phenomenon. During heavy shelling of the Battalion's trenches near Zonnebeke: *'... the harmful effects of fumes from the enemy shells were first noticed'*, and then four days later: *'The fumes from the shells again affected the men and, in some cases, rendered them unconscious'*. The utter awfulness of modern industrialised warfare had just become even more terrible.

The grim privations of trench warfare were briefly relieved by a poignant moment of regimental history. As the 2nd Battalion marched through Ypres on 10th April, *en route* to a new position, men of the 1st Battalion, which was stationed in Ypres, lined the road near the medieval Cloth Hall. It was the first time that the Regiment's two senior Battalions had met in the field since their predecessor regiments, the 31st and 70th Regiments of Foot, had served together in the French Revolutionary Wars of the late 18th Century.

But the 2nd Battalion was about to be pitched into another bloodbath. On the 26th and 27th April, in what is now known as the Second Battle of Ypres, 141 men were killed and 256 wounded. A week later, a further 100 were killed and 133 wounded. On 2nd May, the War Diary records:

> *'... a veil of greenish-yellow gas was plainly seen from our position hanging over the*

> trench line where the attack was taking place'.

The Battalion was not to remain a spectator in this new form of chemical warfare for very long. On 24th May:

> 'About 3.00am the whole line held by the battalion was heavily gassed with asphyxiating gases (...) 'C' Company retired and no trace of it (about 100 men) has yet been found'.

Casualties were listed as five killed, 19 wounded, 157 missing and 24 *'suffering from gas poisoning'*.

The long summer continued, with the Battalion alternating between trench duty and periods of time behind the line in billets. The Diary records the arrival of a steady flow of reinforcements to make good the losses that had been suffered, but also indicates that the Battalion continued to take casualties in a way that the entries imply had become merely routine. For example, the entry for the period 4th to 7th June records: *'Two killed, one wounded. Nothing important happened. Everything exceptionally quiet'*.

The first half of September 1915 found the Battalion in billets at Dranoutre, enduring persistent heavy rain, alternating with periods of trench duty at Wulverghem. On 22nd September the Battalion was marched to billets at Strazerle, with orders to be ready to move again at very short notice. The order duly came on 26th September, with the Battalion moving into the trenches at Vermelles via Bethune to take part in the first phase of the battle of Loos. This action involved a concerted attack on the Hohenzollern Redoubt, which was regarded by Allied military planners as the strongest German position on the whole of the Western Front. This was the action in which Lieut. Fleming-Sandes won his VC on 29th September. The Battalion fought a dogged defensive action against heavy German assaults to hold the position that Lieut. Fleming-Sandes' gallantry had helped to secure. On the 30th, the Diary reports: *'Furious bombing continued all day in the Redoubt, but the Battalion held on to its original position until relieved at 7.00am on 1st October'.*

Once again, the Battalion had suffered very heavy casualties, and following its relief it was ordered into billets for rest, refitting and training, with only occasional short periods of duty in the reserve trenches.

Then, on 21st October, without any prior warning, orders were received for the Battalion to march to the railway station at Porquereuil the next day to entrain for the Mediterranean port of Marseilles, from where they were to sail to Egypt. Having been brought all the way from India in December 1914 for service on the Western Front, the Battalion had now been assigned to the Salonika Expeditionary Force. And in the intense heat of the Macedonian summer the malarial mosquito was to prove every bit as deadly as the enemy's bullets and artillery shells.

--ooOoo--

Chapter 5

April 1915: The Defence of Hill 60

On 20th and 21st April 1915, during the second battle of Ypres, the 1st Battalion of the East Surrey Regiment played a leading part in an action known as 'The Defence of Hill 60'. Hill 60, located around three miles south-east of Ypres in Belgium and known locally as 'Côte des Amants' ('Lovers' Hill') was actually an enormous mound of spoil that had been removed during the 19th century construction of the nearby railway line. Because it was an area of elevated land in an otherwise entirely flat landscape, the hill had an obvious strategic importance in the battles for the exposed salient around the eastern side of Ypres. In this short but desperate action the Battalion's subsequent tally of gallantry medals amounted to an extraordinary three Victoria Crosses, two Military Crosses and seven Distinguished Conduct Medals.

The War Diary records that April 15th was *'... a fine day'*, which saw the Battalion withdrawn to the Ypres Cavalry Barracks for a period of rest and recuperation, having endured several days of heavy German shelling in the front-line trenches. Between

12th and 15th April, the Battalion had lost eight other ranks killed, with seventeen more men wounded. A detachment of eighteen reinforcements arrived on the 15th. The following day was spent in improving the sanitary arrangements in the Barracks, which had evidently been in a poor state when the Battalion arrived.

But it was to be only a fleeting period of calm before the storm. On April 17th, Hill 60, which was then in German hands, was blown up in a massive explosion by the recently-formed Royal Engineers. The Battalion was ordered to be ready to receive enemy prisoners (the Diary records that one German officer and sixteen other ranks came in) and then to move into positions on what was left of the hill. On the late afternoon of the 18th it duly moved up, without suffering any casualties. The Diary describes the text-book positions that the Battalion's four companies took up on the ravaged ground:

> 'A Coy. and ¼ of C Coy. held the front trenches on the Hill, the other ¼ of C Coy. held trenches on right of hill up to and including the railway. ¼ of D Coy. were in support immediately behind the hill. The remaining ¼ D Coy. held fire trenches on the

> *left of Hill. B Coy, held fire and support trenches on left of D Coy. The Machine Gun Detachment had 5 guns mounted in the front line, one in C Coy's trench, covering the right flank of hill; 4 in D & B Coys, fire trenches sweeping ground on left and front of hill.'*

The Battalion immediately came under artillery attack, aimed especially at the support trenches and communications. The barrage intensified, and at 5.00pm the Diary records that ....

> *'... the Germans opened a very heavy bombardment of all the trenches which lasted for an hour but no infantry attack materialised. The trenches were badly damaged and the rest of the night was spent in repairing the damage and improving the communication between the hill and supports. In spite of continual shelling and bombing throughout the night the men worked magnificently and all damage had been repaired by the morning.'*

But this was just the beginning. Heavy shelling resumed at 11.00am, with deadly accuracy and, as the Diary records, *'... trenches were blown in and many men were killed and buried.'* From this point, the diarist's graphic account needs no embellishment:

> 'During this time Capt. & AdJt. Wynyard seeing some men attending wounded men near a shelled spot, went towards them, moved the men along the trench away from the danger spot, attended the wounded himself and in doing so was blown to bits. During this time the Germans were crawling up their old communication trenches and flinging bombs in to fire trenches, but could make no headway owing to our hand grenades and rifle fire. On the death of Capt. Wynyard, Major Paterson, the Comdg. Officer, sent for 2 Lt. Dymott to take over the duties of Adjutant, temporarily. About 2 p.m. Capt. Wynter, Comdg. E Coy. went forward on to the hill to reconnoitre the trenches held by A Coy. Before taking over after dark. During this reconnaissance he was wounded in the leg, and placed in a dug-out for shelter; soon afterwards the dug-out was hit by a shell which caused Capt. Wynter's death. About 3 p.m. the Germans in front of Coy. attempted to assault that trench, but on rising from their trench were hurled back by hand grenades and rifle fire. In this action,

Pte. Dwyer, D Coy. greatly distinguished himself by crawling up the parapet and flinging hand grenades at the enemy, he himself being under a perfect hail of enemy bombs. About this time Lt. Watson who was in the support trench was killed by a heavy howitzer shell. About 3.30 p.m. Lt. Darwell, the Machine Gun Officer, was sent for by the Comdg. Officer to go to Bn. Headqtrs to take over the duties of Adjutant to the Battn. On arrival there he found Major Paterson, the Com Officer, killed, and that 2 Lt. Dymott had been seriously wounded and carried to the dressing station. Now a most terrific bombardment of the position commenced, which lasted for two hours, the hill during this time being a mass of smoke flame and debris. The enemy employed shells giving off asphyxiating gases freely. The result of this was every telephone line to the rear was out and communication with the Artillery and Sector Headqrs made impossible. By this time, every man from the support trenches had been sent to reinforce the fire trenches on the hill and still more men were wanted. In taking up these supports 2nd Lt. Norton was killed by a heavy howitzer in the communication trench. Lieut. Roupell. wounded in several places succeeded in reaching Sector Headqrs when the bombardment was at its height, and explained to Colonel Griffith, Comdg. Sector the situation, asking for reinforcements. Corpl. Harding, the Battn. Signaling Corpl. also managed to deliver a message asking for reinforcements to Sector Headqrs. An orderly was sent with the S.O.S. signal to the Artillery Observing station on the "Dump". The reinforcements arrived about 6 p.m. and Major Allison, 1st Bedford, took over command of the hill position. The bombard of front line lasted to about this hour and after this all their Artillery fire was directed against reserve and support trenches and lines of approach: this continued well into the night, and abated somewhat about midnight. Throughout the night until 3 a.m. the enemy repeatedly assaulted our trenches on the hill with bombs, only once did they succeed in gaining a footing and then they were immediately driven out. Once during the night the enemy attempted to assault the trench held by B Coy. but were immediately driven back by rifle fire. Lateral

> *telephonic communication between Coys., was restored about 10 p.m. from 3 to 6 a.m. the situation was much quieter.'*

At 6.00am. the following morning, the East Surrey's position on the Hill was taken over by the Devon Regiment. But it was not the end of the dying. The Diary records that:

> *'... 2nd Lieut Davis, who was with his Coy. all through the night on the hill, was killed as he was being relieved. Capt. Huth was killed on the night of the 19th whilst superintending work on the trench hold by his Coy.'*

The War Diary describes the deeply poignant conclusion to this action:

> *'After relief the Battn, now under command of Lt. T. H. Darwell, marched to billets at KRUISSTRAAT bringing with it the body of the Comdg. Officer, Major Paterson, which was interred later on in the day in the Convent grounds YPRES'.*

During the morning, the Diary records that a message was received from Colonel Thesiger, the Commanding Officer of the 14th Infantry Brigade. The Colonel wrote: *"Deeply deplore loss of your C.O., so many Officers and men but congratulate the*

Battn. on the gallant example they have set to all". The Battalion was ordered to march to Ouderom for the Army Corps Commander-in-Chief's parade.

> *'At about 9.00am the Army Corps Comdr. visited Battn. said how he deplored the Battn's losses and congratulated Battn. on its fine performance, adding "it was the most magnificent thing yet in the whole war". He also pointed out Sir John French's praise and satisfaction that the German's should realize what British morale would stand. Afterwards he addressed the Sergt. Major and told him how Sir John French has asked who was holding the front-line trenches on the Hill and when told the East Surreys said 'Thank God the East Surreys are there'. He asked the Sergt. Major to Let the NCOs know this. Battn. marched to Hutments at OUDERDOM at 11.30 a.m. and at 2.50 p.m. paraded in field close by with other units which had taken part in the fight on Hill 60 where Sir J. French addressed the troops on their glorious achievement. Orders received from 5th Divn to stand by.'*

The three gallant soldiers who won the Victoria Cross at Hill 60, Private Edward Dwyer, 2nd

Lieutenant (later Major) Benjamin Handley Geary and Lt (later Brigadier) George Rowland Patrick Roupell, are each commemorated by a plaque in the Holy Trinity Chapel in All Saints Church.

--ooOoo--

Chapter 6

July 1st 1916 - Into Battle with Footballs!

The East Surrey Regiment raised seven Service battalions during World War I, initially from volunteers and then after December 1915 from conscripts. These Service battalions formed part of what became known as 'Kitchener's Army', properly the 'New Army'. The Regiment's 7th, 8th, 9th 12th and 13th Service Battalions all served in France. As the Regimental History observes:

> 'These non-Regular battalions had fine fighting records, and in every way maintained the traditions of the Regiment, enhancing its prestige by their gallantry and endurance. All of them took part in the battle of the Somme in 1916, and showed themselves as worthy members of the Regiment whose proud name they bore.'

On the notorious first day of the battle of the Somme, 1st July 1916, the 8th (Service) Battalion took part in the 55th Brigade's attack on Montauban Ridge, which lies between the river Somme to the south and the Albert-Bapaume road to the north. The men had endured a long night of enemy shelling as they waited in the front-line trenches, losing three men killed and ten wounded even before the attack had begun. An intense British artillery bombardment of the German front lines had been intended to clear the way for the dawn infantry attack, which, it was envisaged by the commanders, would simply advance at walking pace across No Man's Land and take possession of the presumably defenceless German trenches. But that was not the way events unfolded. The Battalion War Diary takes up the story:

> *'At 7.27am 'B' Company started to move out to their wire, Captain Neville strolling quietly ahead of them, giving an occasional order to keep the dressing square on to the line of advance. The Company took four footballs out with them which they were seen to dribble forward into the smoke of our intense bombardment on the Hun front line. The first part of the advance was made with very few casualties, but when the barrage lifted to the second Hun trench, a very heavy rifle and machine gun fire started from our front and left, coming apparently from the craters and the high ground immediately behind them.'*

All along the 15-mile line of the British attack, the preliminary artillery barrage had failed in its purpose. The German defences proved to be very much intact, and their ferocious resistance resulted in the highest level of casualties ever experienced by the British army in a single day: 20,000 men dead and 40,000 wounded or missing, with a staggering 60% of all the officers involved on the first day being killed.

Yet despite heavy rifle and machine gun fire from craters and higher ground to its left, by 7.50am the 8th Battalion had somehow reached the first line of German trenches, where, as the Diary reports, *'hand to hand fighting went on for a long time'*. At 10.00am, the Adjutant reported to Brigade HQ that the village of Pommiers, the Battalion's preliminary objective, had been reached but that since heavy casualties had been sustained, further advance would not be possible without reinforcements. Duly supplemented by three companies of the West Kent Regiment, the attack was resumed, and the road to the west of Montauban was reached by mid-day. Still under heavy German artillery fire and continuing to take casualties, the East Surreys, along with detachments from the Buffs and the West Kents, set about consolidating their position. The

War Diary records a moment of touching humanity amidst all the carnage:

> '... later L/C Brame turned up with a bottle of champagne (which) was sent round from officer to officer (listing nine by name) …. in fact all the East Surrey officers engaged in the attack who had not been killed or wounded'

Later in the afternoon, with the Battalion still enduring heavy artillery fire (the Diary comments, somewhat inadequately in the dire circumstances, that *'it was hard to know where to put the men for safety'*) a party of Suffolks arrived with twenty-five canvas buckets of water *'which were extremely welcome'*.

The Battalion was relieved by the West Kents during the night, but because of the heavy fire it was not able to withdraw to the rear trenches until 4.30am on the morning of July 2nd. The Diary records a grim situation:

> 'The men were dog tired and there was nowhere else for them to lie except in the bottom of the trench. Carrying parties coming up and wounded and returning

> *parties coming down all tried to force a passage'.*

Later, the men were moved back to huts in Carnoy Valley, but as the Diary laconically observes:

> *'...the advantages of this position were somewhat lessened by the fact that two 60-pounder artillery batteries had been placed so that they fired just clear of the tops of the huts, from only a few yards behind them.'*

And later, in a melancholy conclusion:

> *'Volunteers from each company went up to the Battle Field to bring in our dead officers, this being done by dark'.*

The Battalion was one of the few British units to reach and hold its objective on that dreadful day, and won two DSOs, two MCs, two DCMs and nine Military Medals for its part in the action. But the gallant Captain Nevill and many of his men were killed during the advance, along with a further 147 of the Battalion's officers and men, with 279 men wounded.

'B' Company's 'Football Attack' was widely reported and caught the national imagination, providing a rare 'good news' story on a day of otherwise almost unmitigated disaster for the Allied cause. The 'Illustrated London News' published a water-colour of the 'football charge' by Richard Caton Woodville Jr on 27th July1916, entitled *The Surreys Play the Game'*. It was accompanied by an anonymous poem called *'An Incident in the Great War: The Game'* which, although it strikes as being distinctly mawkish by today's standards, would undoubtedly have struck a patriotic chord in 1916. The poem begins:

On through the hail of slaughter,
Where gallant comrades fall,
Where blood is poured like water,
They drive the trickling ball.
The fear of death before them,
Is but an empty name;
True to the land that bore them,
The Surrey's play the game.
On without check or falter,
They press towards the goal.

The precise number of footballs involved in the episode is a matter of some dispute. The War Diary, and also a report in the Daily Telegraph on 12th July 1916, state that four footballs were kicked over during the charge, whilst other contemporary sources insist that there were only two. But in any event, one of the footballs was exhibited in the Regimental Museum at Clandon Park House until the catastrophic fire of 2015 which completely destroyed the museum and almost its entire contents, including the venerable football. A (perhaps *the*) second football is exhibited in The Princess of Wales's Royal Regiment and the Queen's Regiment Museum at Dover Castle.

--ooOoo--

Chapter 7

The East Surrey Regiment on November 11th 1918

When war was declared in August 1914, the East Surrey Regiment consisted of just two regular battalions: the 1st Battalion, stationed in Ireland but very rapidly deployed to Belgium as part of the British Expeditionary Force, and the 2nd Battalion, stationed in India but recalled to England in December 1914 for subsequent deployment to France in February 1915.

During the course of the war, the Regiment expanded to nineteen battalions, comprising along with the two Regular battalions and two Special Reserve battalions, four Territorial Army and twelve 'New Army' (or 'Special Service') units, including four London Regiment battalions that were 'cap badged' to the East Surrey Regiment. By the end of the war, some of the special Service battalions had been disbanded and their men dispersed to other East Surrey formations. The 7th, for example, was disbanded in February 1918 as part of a major army reorganization and dispersed to the 8th, 9th and 13th Battalions, whilst the 15th Battalion was formed in

March 1918 only to be absorbed into the 13th just four months later.

The various Battalion War Diaries show that when the Armistice was signed at 11.00am on 11th November 1918, nine battalions of the East Surrey Regiment were deployed on active service, mainly in Europe but also in the Middle East. A tenth battalion, the 1/6th, had returned to its station in India after having spent a year on garrison duty in the Aden Settlement, protecting the territory against the threat of Turkish invasion.

The 1st Battalion was stationed on the Somme. It was in the process of being withdrawn from the front line after weeks of fierce fighting, and on the 11th November was marching from Pont-sur-Sambre to Le Quesney, which had involved a 6.30am start. The Battalion's final casualties of the war (four other ranks killed, and two officers and 37 'Other Ranks' wounded) had been sustained between November 4th and 7th. Strangely, the Battalion War Diary makes no mention of the Armistice on 11th November, but on the next day it records that following an inspection by the Commanding Officer:

> '...a large quantity of new clothing is required, many suits at present in possession of the men are badly torn'.

The 2nd Battalion was stationed in Salonika, where it had been opposing Bulgarian forces. On 1st November, the day on which Bulgaria (and also Turkey) surrendered to the Allies, the War Diary records that the Battalion was in the village of Guvesne, near Salonika *'... standing by for a move'*. The move proved to be a deployment to join the Allied occupation of Constantinople. Following a route march to Summer Hill Camp, the main British Depot in Salonika, where the Brigade Commander praised their marching and appearance, new kit was drawn from the stores and surplus transport handed in, leaving the Battalion, as the Diary puts it, *'immobile'*. But not for long. On 11th November the Battalion embarked on the troopship HMT 'Katsomba' for Constantinople, where on 15th November they occupied forts on the European shore of the Bosphorus. The Armistice is not mentioned in the Diary.

The 1/5th Battalion, one of the East Surrey's Territorial Army units, was deployed in Mesopotamia (modern-day Iraq) on 11th November and was encamped at Lesser Zab on the banks of the river Tigris, occupied in repairing the vital north-south railway line. The Diary had recorded on 1st November: *'All hostilities with Turkey to cease. An Armistice has been signed by Turkey. No more forward movements to be made.* Now, on 11th November, at 10.00am, the diarist records: *'Received news of Armistice with Germany. Great rejoicings'*. And then it was back to repairing the railway line!

The response of the 8th Battalion to the news of the Armistice was more animated:

> *'At 09.30, a message was received to the effect that hostilities would cease at 11.00 hours ... the Battalion band paraded and two bugles sounded the 'Stand Fast', the Band marching up and down the village playing the 'Marseillaise' followed by large crowds of men of the various units billeted in the village'.*

The Battalion was in northern France, billeted at Pommereuil, following fierce fighting earlier in the month. By a grim historical irony, Pommereuil was very near Le Cateau, where the 1st Battalion had been involved in the dogged fighting retreat from Mons in August 1914.

Meanwhile, the 9th Battalion was at Le Plssotiau, in northern France, marching back from the Front having been relieved by the 12th Battalion of the Kings Royal Rifle Corps (KRRC). On 10th November, the Battalion had been marching down the Mons to

Maubeurge road when a German shell exploded amongst them, killing three horses, wounding eight men and killing the Regimental Sergeant Major of the KRRC. The march was continued on 11th November. The War Diary entry for the day records:

> *'At 5.30am the Battalion moved off, and on the way, news was received that the enemy had accepted the terms of our Armistice. The men hardly credited the news (...) In the afternoon, the CO had the Battalion paraded and addressed a few words to them (and) thanked them for their splendid work'.*

The 12th Battalion was on the move from billets in Harlesbeke, Belgium, having crossed the river Scheldt near Berchem, following action on the Cambrai-Essaut Canal. The War Diary entry for 11th November simply reads: *'Signing of Armistice was announced at 10.30. Divine Service held at 18.00'.* The following day is described as: *'...a quiet day: sports and concerts were arranged'.*

Three further Battalions, the 1/21st, the 1/23rd, and the 2/23rd, London Regiment units assigned to the East Surrey Regiment, were in Belgium at the time of the Armistice, taking part in a general advance across the country towards the German border. The 1/21st were in billets at Dime, near Tournai, with orders to continue moving forward. The War Diary records that the order was cancelled on the morning of 11th November, and the Battalion returned to its billets. The 1/23rd Battalion, at Frasnes, was paraded at 9.30am of 11th November, ready to march to Kain as part of the general advance. During the march, at 11.00am, the Diary simply notes:

> *'News received that the German delegation had signed the Armistice terms. No demonstration ensued'.*

The 2/23rd was also involved in the general advance through Belgium, moving forward from Ploen. On 11th November, the War Diary notes:

> *'At 10.30 hours news was received that an Armistice has been signed with Germany and that hostilities should cease at 11.00 hours. However, the advance was confirmed and the Battalion marched to Ellezelles'.*

And so the *'War That Will End All War'*, as H. G. Wells had idealistically characterized the conflict at its outset, was over. But it was at a terrible cost: the total military and civilian casualties of the War have been reliably estimated at 40 million. And amongst this incomprehensible number are the 6,684 men of the East Surrey Regiment, many of them local to the Kingston area, who did not come home.

With hostilities at an end, the British government was confronted with a huge political and logistical challenge. An enormous, and an enormously expensive, fighting force, consisting substantially of volunteers and conscripts, was deployed in Europe, the Middle East, Turkey and in several other theatres, but with no fighting to do. Just how was this force to be managed in the weeks and months following the Armistice, and when (and indeed how) was it to be brought home? Some of the East Surrey Regiment's Territorial and Service Battalions would be disbanded quite soon after the War, whilst others were destined to become part of the Army of Occupation of the Rhineland. The 2nd Battalion was briefly involved in the occupation of Constantinople until its return to Kingston in April 1919, after which it was deployed to Egypt in April 1920. The 1st Battalion, after a short respite back in England, soon found itself in action once again as part of the four-Battalion-strong British contribution to the Allied Expeditionary Force that was dispatched to Russia in 1919 to support the beleaguered Tsarist forces against the insurgent Bolsheviks.

--ooOoo--

Chapter 8

1919: The East Surreys in Russia

A small military cemetery maintained by the Commonwealth War Graves Commission in Murmansk, a port city in the far north of Russia in an inlet of the Barents Sea and 200 miles north of the Arctic Circle, contains the graves of six soldiers of the 1st Battalion, East Surrey Regiment. The simple headstones of these graves record the dates of their deaths as having been between 1st September and 15th September 1919. This was almost a year after the Armistice had brought an end to the First World War. How this remote cemetery became yet another 'far corner of a foreign field' is part of the story of a British military operation that has been almost entirely forgotten.

The Russian Revolution of November 1917 resulted in the Bolshevik ('Red') faction seizing power. The new revolutionary government hastily signed a peace treaty with the Central Powers (Germany and its allies) and killed Tsar Nicholas, together with the Tsarina and their children. The vast country split into mutually antagonistic loyalist 'White' and revolutionary 'Red' factions and descended into civil war. The British government became increasingly drawn into the conflict. What had begun as a small-scale deployment of Royal Marines to Murmansk in March 1918 that was intended to protect a large stockpile of Allied-donated war materials quickly escalated. 'Mission creep' saw the British government effectively pursuing a war against the Bolsheviks on a number of fronts, in support of British-trained and equipped 'White Russian' forces. This 'post-war' campaign has almost completely faded from the national memory. As Damien Wright has revealed in his extensively researched book *'Churchill's Secret War with Lenin'* (Wright, 2019), following the withdrawal of British forces in mid-1920 the British government 'classified' all official documents relating to the ill-fated adventure, and although these files have since been released, the fact that Britain was once involved in a war against Russia is something that is not commonly known.

The East Surrey Regiment's 1st Battalion was part of the North Russian Expeditionary Force (NREF), and was deployed to Murmansk in 1919 with the tasks of ensuring the security of the vital ice-free port, protecting the strategically important Murmansk to Petrograd (the former St Petersburg) railway line and supporting the White Russian army by driving back the Bolshevik forces as far as possible. The

Regiment had returned to Aldershot in April 1919 following the end of World War I, but by mid-August of the same year it was heading back into action.

Although the NREF operation in which the East Surreys were to be involved was to be the largest undertaken out of Murmansk during the whole period of the short North Russian campaign, it was actually a final strategic 'push' ahead of a complete withdrawal. The political decision to extract all British forces from Russia by the end of 1919 had been taken in London earlier in the year, following an international agreement at the end of the Paris Peace conference. By mid-1919, several Allied governments had withdrawn their contingents from the NREF, seriously depleting its numbers. The East Surreys were in effect being deployed to help shore up a lost cause and to ensure that when the time came for withdrawal, it could be carried out safely and in an orderly fashion.

The Battalion, comprising 34 officers and 718 other ranks together with the Medical Officer and the Chaplain, embarked at Tilbury Docks on HMT 'Kildonan Castle' on the morning of 16th August 1919. Accommodation on board was evidently very tight, as the regimental transport had to be left behind. The officers were allocated cabins whilst the other ranks were accommodated 'below', with an issue of hammocks and blankets. At 3.00pm in the afternoon, the ship set sail down-river towards an anchorage off Gravesend. The Diary records that:

> '... as the vessel was going down the river, ships of every description blew their syrens (sic), and the troops replied with shouts and whistles.'

The ship remained anchored off Gravesend for the next two days, with the promenade deck being put to use for physical training, musketry and rapid loading practice. The Lewis Gun crews received special training from their officers. During the afternoon, the regimental band played on deck. At 5.00pm on the 19th August, the 'Kildonan Castle' weighed anchor and sailed off towards the Nore Lightship, where the anchor was dropped once more. And then, at 9.00pm that evening, as the Diary records, '... the voyage commenced'.

The days of August 20th to the 24th were spent at sea, with routine on-deck training activities maintained throughout the voyage. The Diary records that there was *'rough weather'* on Sunday 24th August, obliging the band to play in the saloon during dinner that evening. On 25th August, the ship docked at Murmansk after what the Diary describes as having been *'a very pleasant voyage'*, with officers and men enjoying *'a very happy time on board.'* The feeding arrangements, the Diary goes on to say *'... had been very good'*. One man had been admitted to hospital during the voyage. Other than that, the whole contingent was reported to be in good health. But the men must have been very cold. They were, after all, 200 miles north of the Arctic Circle.

At 8.00pm, the Battalion disembarked in companies as the band *'... played Selections on the Quay'*, and the Commanding Officer was handed his orders. The troops boarded the two trains that were waiting on the quay and steamed south for the Kapaselga front via Imandra, Belya and Kandelashska, dropping off small contingents of 'D' Company at each halt in order to ensure the security of the Battalion's rear. The trains continued on their journey, departing Kandelashka at 1.00am for Kem, which was reached at 5.15pm. At 11.40am on the 28th August, the trains arrived at the lakeside town of Medjeva Gora, and then one train, carrying just 'A' Company and 'C' Company, together with the Battalion Headquarters staff, continued down the line to the village of Kapaselga. After spending the night on the train, the Battalion relieved the Royal Marine Light Infantry, which was holding the Outpost Line about three miles in front of the village. The War Diary records a textbook deployment, with forward and support positions quickly established and secured. On the 31st August a patrol set out along the railway line to a point five miles ahead of the Outpost Line but, as the Diary records '...*saw nothing of the enemy'*. A map of the area, along with contemporary photographs of the railway and its surroundings near Mumanksk, show a flat and coldly bleak landscape characterised by enormous lakes and dense spruce forests. It was a far cry from the trenches of northern France.

The first week of September was spent in consolidation, training, reconnaissance and repairing damaged railway bridges in anticipation of an advance, always with the very real possibility of enemy intervention. And on September 13th, the Battalion suffered its first casualties of the campaign. Lieutenant R. B. Marshall of 'C' Company was severely wounded when his patrol encountered a forty-strong party of Bolshevik troops some 500 yards ahead of the Outpost position. Lieutenant Marshall, who had been wounded twice whilst serving in France, died of his wounds the next day. After a temporary burial in Kapaselga churchyard, he was subsequently interred in the Cemetery at Murmansk. What the Diary fails to mention is that

Private Horace Terry was also killed in the same action. He is also buried in Murmansk.

Having made first contact with the enemy, the Battalion now prepared for serious action. The Battalion Operation Orders, which are included as appendices in the War Diary, show that the offensive involved the disposition of the NREF forces into two main columns, one advancing down the railway line and the other forcing a way down the road that ran more or less parallel with the line. The East Surreys were almost entirely assigned to the Railway Column. At 6.00am the next day (14th September), 'A' and 'C' Companies began to move forward along the line to engage the enemy's outpost positions, and quickly came under heavy machine gun and rifle fire. The East Surreys took the fusillade in their stride and responded with interest. As the Diary puts it:

> *'This fire was maintained until superiority of fire was obtained...the Battalion advanced ... the enemy then fled from his main position, which was captured at 09.20hrs'.*

The advance continued, with all the Battalion's objectives successfully gained by 22.00hrs that evening, in spite of having had to deal with a burning railway bridge in order to cross the river. This crossing was distinctly hazardous, involving, as the Diary rather casually puts it: *'... the use of a ladder suspended from the centre of the bridge'*. The men then had to work late into the night to prevent the bridge from collapsing and taking the railway line with it. Four men were *'slightly wounded'* during the day's operation, three of them as a result of 'friendly fire' caused by artillery shrapnel which fell short of the intended target.

With the bridge successfully saved, and the railway line consequently unbroken, the advance was resumed by 'D' Company at 7.00am the following morning, September 15th. The enemy was clearly not far away. The Diary records that:

> *'... although no opposition was encountered for a considerable distance, signs were visible of very recent occupation, such as burning fires and food in the course of preparation'.*

Pushing further forward, a lone patrol came under fire. An Outpost Line was established in order to secure the position and two stronger patrols moved out towards the enemy, which was well concealed in and around a small village. The Diary records that the patrols came under heavy machine gun and rifle fire and were held up because they were becoming 'enfiladed' (i.e. attacked from the side of its position) by enemy forces. A captured soldier revealed that four hundred 'Red Finns' had just arrived (the Russian border with Finland was to the west of the conflict zone, and not very far away either) and had immediately been deployed by the Bolsheviks. This was clearly a potentially hazardous situation for the East Surreys, and although an enveloping movement with artillery support was attempted in conjunction with other units it was not wholly successful because of the considerably increased strength of the opposition. The forward troops were consequently withdrawn 400 yards back from the village. An ensuing thirty-minute artillery bombardment of the enemy positions was a prelude to a concerted infantry attack, which was successful in capturing the village and the adjacent railway siding, against only slight opposition. The advance continued to the line of the Chebina River, which was the Battalion's final objective for the day, and where Outposts were established for the night. The Diary concludes the day's entry with a summary of the day's considerable achievements:

> *'A large quantity of war materials was captured, including three trains containing ammunition, machine guns, rifles and transport. Prisoners were also taken. Our*

casualties during the day's operations were three killed and six wounded'.

The advance down the railway line continued the next day (16th September) with 'B' Company in the lead and 'D' Company forming the 'main body', initially meeting only light opposition. The advance guard reached Siding 4, where it came under persistent heavy fire from nearby high ground. The Diary records that at the same time, the sound of heavy artillery, machine gun and rifle fire was heard from the direction of the Road Column, and a platoon was assigned to work round a nearby village in order to attack the rear of the Bolshevik position.

This relief operation commenced at 17.30 hours, with the platoon attacking the enemy positions with Lewis gun and rifle fire. This intervention was a complete success, enabling the Road Column to resume its advance and to link up with the relieving platoon. The Diary records that *'... the platoon took 25 prisoners and killed many of the enemy'.*

After fierce fighting throughout the remainder of the day, the Bolshevik troops were finally driven from their positions and the Battalion was able to advance to its final objective, reaching it at 22.00hrs. The diary notes that twelve prisoners were taken during the operation *'...making a total of 120 prisoners taken during the whole advance'.* The Battalion's casualties during the day were one officer and four other ranks wounded. The new position was consolidated in depth, and there were no further Bolshevik attacks. This was to be the limit of the advance. Two days later, reconnaissance patrols reported that the village of Zapolki in front of the Outpost positions '...*was clear of the enemy and the villagers were friendly'*. A second patrol to the nearby village of Pavolitski found that the whole area was also clear of the enemy. The strategic objective of inflicting a severe blow on the Bolshevik forces and driving them back as far as possible had been achieved, and with a very low level of casualties on the British side.

On the morning of September 21st, the Battalion was relieved by units of the North Russian Rifle Regiment, and later in the day entrained for the return journey to Medveja Gora. On September 24th, the Diary poignantly records that:

> *'... The bodies of the three men who were killed during the attack on Siding 5 on September 15th were exhumed and sent back to Kapesega for burial in the British Cemetery.'*

The northward rail journey continued during the next few days, and the final Diary entry, on September 30th, records the Battalion embarking on *HMS Mirana* at Murmansk, which would take them back to the UK and to barracks at Ripon in North Yorkshire. But it was to be a very brief respite. In January 1920 the Battalion was posted to Dublin for what were officially described as 'Internal Security Operations' against the insurgent Irish republicans. It was, of course, from Dublin that the Regiment had set out for France in August 1914, as part of the British Expeditionary Force. The wheel of fortune had turned full circle.

The East Surrey's contribution to the NREF campaign had unquestionably been a conspicuous success. All of its objectives had been taken, with only light casualties sustained during the operation, and undoubtedly a serious blow had been dealt to the Bolshevik forces both in terms of men and materials lost and of territory conceded. The White Russian army was left in a comparatively strong position. But it was not to last. The Whites were heavily outnumbered, riven by internal disputes, riddled with corruption, and were now without international support. Barely five months after the British withdrawal, and even before the harsh north Russian winter had ended, Murmansk had fallen to

Bolshevik forces and the White Russian resistance collapsed.

The personal diary of Captain R.E.C. Adams MC, 2nd-in-command of 'C' Company, which is held by the Surrey Infantry Museum, provides a wry judgement on the ultimate futility of the expedition:

> *'I have never been more pleased at the prospect of leaving any country than I am this one. The attraction of France and Belgium was often rather subtle and frequently not noticeable at all, but at all events the campaign was a going concern with a sound cause and working to a definite end. Here you could not help thinking you were a third party dumped in the middle of a particularly apathetic civil war, in which neither side knew what they were fighting for but equally did not know how to stop fighting. (....) In leaving them to fight it out, one can only wish them good luck and may the best man win.'*[2]

--ooOoo--

---

[2] Adams, Capt. R.E.C.: *North Russia*. Surrey Infantry Museum.

Conclusion

"Well, I thought the same as everybody else. Everybody said 'It'll be over by Christmas and you've got to get out there soon, otherwise you won't see anything'. But I don't know if it was my opinion, or if everybody was saying it. One certainly changed one's mind when we found out how well organised Jerry was compared with us, for instance. And how thinly we were on the ground, of course"[3]

It soon became apparent that it would not be over by Christmas, nor anything remotely like it. The battle of the Marne in September 1914 succeeded in checking the German advance on Paris. But the subsequent failure later in the same month to dislodge the Germans from their defensive positions at the battle of Aisne, followed by the failure of the battle of Loos of in September and October 1915 to achieve a decisive breakthrough, led to a long period of attritional trench warfare that did not end until the deadlock was broken at the battle of Cambrai in November 1917. Even then, the Allied armies had to withstand a series of massive German assaults which began in March 1918 and were not finally

---

[3] *'Voices of the First World War'*, Imperial War Museum.

halted until mid-July. The offensive came perilously close to succeeding, and only when it had been repulsed could the Allies sweep across Belgium with the German army in headlong retreat before them. Political and economic collapse in Germany led to the negotiation of the Armistice, which came into effect at 11.00am on 11th November 1918.

The East Surreys were there from the beginning to the end, and (taking the 1st Battalion's involvement in the 1919 North Russian campaign into account) well beyond the end too. The two Regular battalions that went into action in August 1914 and January 1915 respectively were supplemented during the four long years of warfare by a huge number of volunteers and conscripts. During the course of the war, the Regiment expanded to comprise over twenty battalions, and the Kingston Barracks saw 87,000 recruits, many of them local men, pass through its gates between 1914 and 1917.

In 1921, the 15th Century Guild Chapel of the Holy Trinity in All Saints Church, Kingston-upon-Thames was dedicated by the Bishop of Southwark as The East Surrey Regiment Memorial Chapel, having been extensively restored by the relatives, friends and comrades of the Regiment in memory of those who had died in the First World War. The Memorial

Gates, which stand at the Market Place entrance to the Churchyard, were dedicated in 1924. The gates were refurbished to mark the centenary of the end of the War, and were re-dedicated on Armistice Day 2018, Sunday November 11th, during a Civic Service led by the Bishop of Kingston and attended by a detachment of the Princess of Wales Royal Regiment, the successor formation to the East Surrey Regiment.

The East Surrey Regiment Memorial Gates Rededication Service, Sunday 11th November 2018[4]

---

[4] Photo: Alastair Deller.

Sources

Books

Adams, Capt. R.E.C.: *North Russia*. Surrey Infantry Museum Ref. ESR/25/ADAMR/1, 1920.

Crowley, Col. Patrick: *The Regimental Chapels of Surrey's Infantry Regiments*. A Princess of Wales Royal Regiment Historical Supplement, 2019.

Daniell, David Scott: *History of the East Surrey Regiment (Vol 4) 1920-1952*. Ernest Benn, London, 1957.

Hastings, Max: *Catastrophe: Europe Goes to War, 1914*. London, Collins, 2014.

Kershaw, Ian: *To Hell and Back: Europe 1914-1949*. Penguin, 2016.

Macdonald, Lyn: *Somme*. Penguin, 1983.

Mallinson, Allan: *1914: Fight the Good fight. Britain, the Army and the Coming of the First World War*. London, Bantam Press, 2014.

Pearce, Col. H. W. & Sloman, Brig. Gen. H. S.: *History of the East Surrey Regiment, Vol. 3 1917-1919*. Naval & Military Press, 2005.

Stevenson, David: *1914-1918: The History of the First World War*. Penguin, 2004.

Stone, Norman: *World War One: A Short History*. Penguin, 2008.

Tuchmann, Barbara: *August 1914*. Papermac, 1994.

Wright, Damien: *Churchill's Secret War with Lenin: British and Commonwealth Intervention in the Russian Civil War, 1918-20*. Helion, 2017.

Websites

Queens Royal Surrey Regiment (Battalion War Diaries): *queensroyalsurreys.org.uk/war_diaries_home_new.shtml*

The National Archives: *nationalarchives.gov.uk/pathways/firstworldwar/spotlights/allies.hlm*

BBC History Extra: *'Britain's Russian Fiasco: The Allied Intervention in the Russian Civil War': historyextra.com/period/20th-century-british-russian-fiasco-allied-intervention-russia.*

Imperial War Museum: *iwm.org.uk/VoicesOfTheFirstWorldWar.*

Imperial War Museum: *iwm.org.uk/collections*
'North Russia Interventions 1918-1920'.

Surrey History Centre, Woking:
https://www.exploringsurreyspast.org.uk/themes/subjects/military/east_surrey_regiments_football_charge_july_1st_1916

APPENDIX

All Saints Church, Kingston upon Thames
The Ancient Parish Church of Kingston

A Service to commemorate the East Surrey Regiment's first engagement of the World War I at the battle of Mons, 23rd August 1914

Saturday 23rd August 2014, 12 noon.

To the Glory of God and in memory

Of the heroic deeds of the 1st East

Surrey Regiment with the first seven

Divisions in 1914 this banner was originally

worked and given for the Commemoration

Festival at the Albert Hall 14th December
1916

(by those who hold their bravery dear)

𝕰𝖆𝖘𝖙 𝕾𝖚𝖗𝖗𝖊𝖞

𝖃𝖃𝖃𝕴

𝕬𝖚𝖌𝖚𝖘𝖙 – 𝕹𝖔𝖛 1914

Hymn: Praise my soul the King of heaven

Praise, my soul, the King of heaven;
to his feet thy tribute bring;
ransomed, healed, restored, forgiven,
evermore his praises sing:
Alleluia, alleluia!
Praise the everlasting King.

Praise him for his grace and favour
to our fathers in distress;
praise him still the same for ever,
slow to chide and swift to bless:
Alleluia, alleluia!
Glorious in his faithfulness.

Father-like, he tends and spares us;
well our feeble frame he knows;
in his hand he gently bears us,
rescues us from all our foes.
Alleluia, alleluia!
Widely yet his mercy flows.

Angels, help us to adore him;
ye behold him face to face;
sun and moon, bow down before him,
dwellers all in time and space.
Alleluia, alleluia!
Praise with us the God of grace.

Welcome and opening prayer: Rev Ken Walker (John Bunyan Baptist Minister and a member of the Ministry Team at All Saints Church)

Reading: The Battalion War Diary 21st to 23rd August 1914: John Dewhurst (Churchwarden)

When war was declared on 4th August 1914, the 1st Battalion of the East Surrey Regiment was stationed in Dublin as part of the 14th Division. By Wednesday 17th August, the Battalion had sailed to Le Havre at its full wartime establishment of 30 officers and 992 other ranks, having been supplemented by its reservists, and was en route by rail via Amiens to the northern French town of Le Cateau. From there, the Battalion marched north towards the Belgian border. The Battalion War Diary takes up the story:

Friday 21st August: Left billets 6.30 am, marching some 15 miles by mostly by road along Foret de Mormal. Weather conditions close and muggy, the march proving very trying to the Reservists.

Saturday 22nd August: Left billets at Bermeries at 7.15am. Crossed Belgian frontier about 9:00am, and marching via Flouges reached the Mons–Conde Canal about 3:00pm after a hot march of some 18 miles made more trying by the cobbled roads of Belgium. The Battalion held the right half of the line from the Canal railway bridge just north-west of Les Herbieres to the Ville Pommeroeul Road, with the Duke of Cornwall Light Infantry the Outpost position of the 14th Brigade and the King's Own Scottish Borderers of the 13th Brigade continuing the Outpost line on our right.

Sunday 23rd August: The morning opened misty and wet, clearing about 10.00 am. Construction of fire trenches continued and clearing of foreground north of Canal commenced, tools for this purpose not arriving previous night. Owing to the houses on the north of the Canal running down to railway bridge, C Company was obliged to hold advanced position on north bank, so it was decided to move A Company up in their immediate support on the south bank, the whole of this section under Maj. H. S. Tew. Two Companies of the Suffolk Regiment were ordered up in reserve about noon. One of these were sent over Canal to assist in clearing the foreground, but owing to the advance of the Germans about 1.00 pm all work had to cease and most of this Company was drawn into the fire trenches along with C Company. The attack was soon pressed and several casualties quickly occurred in this section, including Capt. J. P. Benson, dangerously wounded. All posts were ordered to offer as much resistance as possible and adjoining posts mutually arranged accordingly with one another, but the Battalion on the left had already been ordered to take up a fresh position further south. By 3.00 pm. The attack was being pressed all along the line and A Coy was now absorbed into the firing line. The Machine Gun section from its position on the railway bridge did excellent work, and coupled with the steady firing of the men in the trenches helped much with to delay the enemies advance. About 6.00 pm the enemy's guns at short range blew in the K.O.S. Borderers' barricade, compelling them to withdraw south of Canal. This enabled the enemy to enfilade our right section which in turn also withdrew south of the Canal, covered by A Company. About 7.00 pm the railway bridge which had previously been prepared for destruction was blown up. This was the pre-arranged signal for the road bridge held by B Company to be also blown up. This was effected none too soon, as the last man had only just left the house loophole and prepared for defence at the bridge head when an enemy shell destroyed it. The withdrawal to the south of the River Haime was then, in accordance with previous instructions received, carried out in good order by alternate positions of the line and covered finally by the remainder of the Suffolk Company. After reporting to Brigade Headquarters at Thulin the Battalion marched to Bois de Boussu where it eventually bivouacked about 2.00 am in a factory yard. Total casualties in this action were 5 Officers and 134 other ranks killed, wounded & missing.

Hymn: Father, hear the prayer we offer

Father, hear the prayer we offer:
not for ease that prayer shall be,
but for strength, that we may ever
live our lives courageously.

Not for ever in green pastures
do we ask our way to be;
but the steep and rugged pathway
may we tread rejoicingly.

Not forever by still waters
would we idly rest and stay;
but would smite the living fountains
from the rocks along our way.

Be our strength in hours of weakness,
in our wanderings be our Guide;
through endeavor, failure, danger,
Saviour, be thou at our side.

Reading: St Paul's letter to the Ephesians, chapter 6, vv 10-17

Finally, be strong in the Lord and in the strength of his power. Put on the whole armour of God, so that you may be able to stand against the wiles of the devil. For our* struggle is not against enemies of blood and flesh, but against the rulers, against the authorities, against the cosmic powers of this present darkness, against the spiritual forces of evil in the heavenly places. Therefore, take up the whole armour of God, so that you may be able to withstand on that evil day, and having done everything, to stand firm. Stand therefore, and fasten the belt of truth around your waist, and put on the breastplate of righteousness. As shoes for your feet put on whatever will make you ready to proclaim the gospel of peace. With all of these,* take the shield of faith, with which you will be able to quench all the flaming arrows of the evil one. Take the helmet of salvation, and the sword of the Spirit, which is the word of God.

Hymn: Who would true valour see

Who would true valour see,
let him come hither;
one here will constant be,
come wind, come weather;
there's no discouragement
shall make him once relent
his first avowed intent
to be a pilgrim.

Whoso beset him round
with dismal stories,
do but themselves confound;
his strength the more is,
No lion can him fright; he'll with a giant fight,
but he will have a right
to be a pilgrim.

Hobgoblin nor foul fiend
can daunt his spirit;
he knows he at the end
shall life inherit.
Then, fancies, fly away;

he'll not fear what men say;
he'll labour night and day to be a pilgrim.

Sermon: Rev Ken Walker

Prayers: read by members of the East Surrey Regimental Association

Collect of The East Surrey Regiment

O God who dost prove and try Thy people as gold is tried in the fire, grant we beseech Thee, of Thy mercy, that Thy servants The East Surrey Regiment, who have been tried by water and by fire and proved in many a day of battle, may never be confounded, for as much as we trust in Thee, through Jesus Christ our Lord. Amen.

Collect of The Queen's Royal Surrey Regimental Association

Lord God of Hosts, Stretch forth, we pray Thee, Thine almighty hand upon all members of the Queen's Royal Surrey Regimental Association. As we give Thee thanks for their dedication and sacrifice through the years, so we pray for them and for all who have striven to preserve peace in their generation. Endue them in every undertaking with courage and loyalty, that at the last, they meet Thee with good spirit and an untroubled heart. This we ask through Jesus Christ, our Lord. Amen.

Prayer of dedication for the Colours before their return to the East Surrey Chapel

Hymn: **O God our help in ages past**

O God, our help in ages past,
our hope for years to come,
our shelter from the stormy blast,
and our eternal home:

Under the shadow of thy throne,
thy saints have dwelt secure;
sufficient is thine arm alone,
and our defence is sure.

Before the hills in order stood,
or earth received her frame,
from everlasting thou art God,
to endless years the same.

A thousand ages in thy sight
are like an evening gone;
short as the watch that ends the night
before the rising sun.

Time, like an ever-rolling stream,
bears all its sons away;
they fly, forgotten, as a dream
dies at the opening day.

O God, our help in ages past,
our hope for years to come,
be thou our guide while troubles last,
and our eternal home!

Blessing

About the Author

A former headteacher, school inspector and university lecturer, John Dewhurst is Head Virger of All Saints Church Kingston upon Thames, where he was a Churchwarden from 2010 to 2016 and again from 2020 to 2025. It was during this time that he became fascinated by the history of the East Surrey Regiment and by the Regiment's many links with the church and the town. He is the author of *'Take One Memorial'* (Amazon Kindle 2025) which tells the story of Lieutenant Francis Edward Blackwood, 1st Battalion East Surrey Regiment, who was killed in action in northern Nigeria in 1906 and who is commemorated in the church.

Printed in Great Britain
by Amazon